MW01592597

COURAGE and COMPASSION: FOLLOWING DOROTHY

An Energy Therapist Explores the Heroine's Journey

Nancy Ann Battilega, LPC, HTCP

Copyright – 2011 by Nancy Battilega

ALL RIGHTS RESERVED

First Edition
Printed in the USA

Book Cover and Illustrations by Deborah Gotto
dgdesigns@qwest.net

Author photograph by Kelly Mulhern
www.kmulhern.com

This book is dedicated to Dorothy Christman Eachus, youngest sister of my mother, Evelyn Mae Christman Scott, with gratitude and appreciation for inspiring this story and for her reminders to open to the heart and stop to smell the roses.

PREFACE

Once upon a time heroines were as rare as a blue moon. Should one chance to appear, it was most likely that her story went untold. Seldom was she regaled in either prose or poetry. The feats of male heroes were celebrated in song and verse. Their episodes form the basis for the traditional liberal arts education: The Iliad, The Odyssey, The Aeneid, the Shakespearean Tragedies, fairy tale heroes, princes, kings and knights too numerous to mention.

History records the exploits of famous women authors and educators, scientists, religious and political leaders. However, until the 20th C., literary heroines were often powerless victims waiting to be rescued by a charming prince. This began to change as more authors, especially female authors, introduced strong, intelligent and courageous female characters into their works.

Until recently, too many women have been unable to answer the call to embark on the heroine's journey. Sensing a lack in education, freedom, money, time or support, they hesitated.

Today, Spirit is calling us to rise above our perceived lack or littleness and claim our birthright.

After authoring a successful book of nursery tales entitled "Father Goose," in 1900 Frank L. Baum wrote a magical story for children featuring a little girl named Dorothy. Beloved throughout the world by adults, as well as children, Dorothy serves as an enchanting role model for our own heroic journeys. Following the lead of her own spirit and instincts, she gains wisdom, love and courage enough to confront her deepest fear and returns home with the ability to transform her environment.

Other authors have referenced Dorothy of Oz as a prototype for the Heroine's Journey. In this book I tell her story from the point of view of a practitioner of energy psychotherapy who views *The Wizard of Oz* as an allegory for the spiritual journey. As Dorothy's chakras (energy centers) expand, she progresses through the stages of the Heroine's Journey until she becomes capable of successfully confronting her shadow and recognizing her true worth.

Table of Contents

DOROTHY and FRIENDS

During twenty years as a therapist, I have often used the story of Dorothy in *The Wizard of Oz* to encourage children and young adults to hang in there through difficult times. This multi-layered story of love, hope and perseverance has thrilled and inspired six generations of readers.

Like so many Americans and others throughout the world, I've seen the 1939 movie version too many times to count, often embarrassing my younger sister by crying when the old neighbor lady captures Toto and rides away with him in her bicycle basket. However, I never really thought about Dorothy in terms of the Heroine's Journey until my own Aunt Dorothy, who passed away many years ago, appeared to me during meditation and suggested I write a story of the Heroine's Journey based on Dorothy of Oz.

During my journey of recovery from breast cancer, I became open to receiving guidance from many sources, including dreams and visions, so I chose to heed Aunt Dorothy. This book is the result of that encounter.

The Heroine's Journey differs from the typical Hero's Journey as depicted in literature. The fundamental difference is, of course, that while the hero must honor his feminine side, the heroine must develop and claim her masculine strengths.

As a mind, body, energy psychotherapist, I am aware that the stages of growth necessary for developing these less dominant strengths parallel the energies contained in the seven chakras These energy centers, aligned from the base of the spine to the crown of the head, govern our physical, emotional and mental functions They also correlate with the seven archetypes of the heroic journey from the innocent orphan, who struggles to survive, to the successful magician, who returns home transformed.

The stages of the heroic journey vary from myth to myth and author to author. Joseph Campbell has written extensively on this subject in *The Hero's Journey* and *The Hero with a Thousand Faces*. Psychoanalyst Robert Johnson further analyzes the hero and heroines' journeys

2

in his classic texts, *He, She & We*.

C.S. Lewis recounts his own version of Psyche's heroic journey of redemption in the powerful *Til We Have Faces*, and Caroline Myss writes extensively about the archetypal patterns of this journey in *Sacred Contracts*.

As I began to think about how I would tell Dorothy's story from this perspective, it seemed obvious to me that Dorothy and her friends represent the development of the chakras and archetypes that underlie the Heroine's Journey.

Chakras are spinning wheels of light that govern the energy centers of the human body. These will be described in detail in Chapter 5. Each of the seven major chakras correlates to one of seven archetypes (personality constellations) typically developed on the heroine's journey.

Dorothy expands the energies of each of these seven chakras and integrates the characteristics of each of the seven archetypes associated with the Heroine's Journey as she travels through Oz.

One of the joys in writing this book is that I was able to pull from so many aspects of my educational and theoretical background in telling the story of Dorothy's heroic journey. I began my educational career as an English major with an emphasis on classical literature and a fascination for heroic lore, Greek mythology and ancient folk and fairy tales.

Early in my counseling career I focused on dream analysis and studied at the Jungian Institute in Zurich. More recently, as I've moved into the integrated, holistic practices of mind, body, energy psychotherapy, I've researched numerology and eastern forms of healing such as acupuncture and acupressure, which work with the chakras and other energy systems of the body. The bibliography lists references for those interested in further information on these topics.

In **The Wizard of Oz,** written in 1900, Frank L. Baum managed to turn the centuries old tale of Psyche's journey into a popular children's book that merges elements of modern energy medicine with the spellbinding storytelling of heroic literature.

Mr. Baum said that he enjoyed making up fairytales for his four sons, nieces and nephews that were fun and entertaining rather than the scary, moralistic tales of his own youth. However, writing Dorothy's story

"was pure inspiration. It came to me right out of the blue. I think that sometimes the Great Author has a message to get across and He has to use the instrument at hand. I happened to be that medium, and I believe the magic key was given to

me to open the doors to sympathy and understanding, joy, peace and happiness." (Hearn, ed., p. xcv)

As Baum realized by acknowledging his debt to Spirit, he has done much more than tell a light-hearted fairy tale about a pleasant little girl. This story conveys the reality of feminine power. During the past hundred years it has become part of what Swiss psychoanalyst, C. J. Jung, termed the "collective unconscious." Clinical psychologist Madonna Kolbenschlag is quoted as saying, *"I have been amazed at the number of times the Dorothy-script surfaces in the consciousness-sometimes in the dreams-of women in transition or undergoing a major transformation in self-image."* (Hearn, p.13)

Like Dorothy, who skipped along the yellow brick road in a pair of silver slippers (until MGM turned them red), we, too, must one day venture forth and face our greatest fears. I believe I chose to do this when I elected non-traditional treatment for breast cancer. My hope, in writing Dorothy's story as the Heroine's Journey, is that many of my readers will feel empowered to choose this "path less traveled" in whatever way is personally appropriate.

The reader will follow Dorothy as she leaves her gray Kansas home, borne through the air in a mass of swirling energy that hints at the transformation to come. Baum's use of color and numerology serves to heighten the tension as Dorothy embarks on her journey-an adventure of external challenges and internal development.

Dorothy's companions assist her on her heroic journey, which is complete only when she integrates their masculine strengths with her feminine grace. The result is a fully developed consciousness that is needed to confront and overcome the Wicked Witch of the West. Only then can Dorothy attempt the return to Aunt Em.

THE JOURNEY BEGINS

 In 1900 Frank L. Baum published the first in a series of Oz books which became known as *The Wizard of Oz*. This story of a little girl named Dorothy, who is transplanted from a Kansas homestead to the magical land of Oz, continues to capture the imagination of the young-at-heart in cultures across the globe.

One reason for its enduring literary presence is the element of adventure faced by the charming heroine and her courageous companions. Another is its modern retelling of the age-old saga of the heroine's journey first recorded in classical Greece as the tale of Cupid and Psyche (Greek for spirit/soul).

I believe Dorothy's story is also an allegory for our inward spiritual journey and, as such, it speaks to the universal spirit, the collective unconscious that joins us all.

Baum prided himself on writing "modernized" fairy tales in an easy to read style that would "amuse and please a child." (Hearn. xxviii) In The Wizard of Oz he succeeds in telling a complex fairy tale using ordinary language. Without resorting to literary gimmicks, he foreshadows the complexity of the story with creative use of colors and numbers.

The first of the Oz books tells the story of orphan, Dorothy Gale, who is lifted with her house and dog, Toto, by a cyclone from the Kansas farm of her Aunt Em and Uncle Henry and dropped, house and all, onto the Wicked Witch of the East in the land of the Munchkins. Here she meets the Good Witch of the South who tells her she must travel along the yellow brick road to Oz where she will meet the wizard, who "may" help her find her way home. The Witch gives Dorothy a pair of silver slippers to help her on her way.

Dorothy's journey is fraught with danger, but she meets three very faithful companions on her way: the Scarecrow who seeks brains; the Tin Woodsman who wants a heart, and the Lion who yearns for courage. The Wizard promises to grant all four travelers their wishes only after they kill the Wicked Witch of the West.

As we follow Dorothy along the yellow brick road we will notice the similarities between her challenges and Psyche's four tasks. We will also note how she expands the seven energy centers along her spine (chakras) and develops the seven archetypes of the heroine's journey, which correspond to each chakra, some of which are represented by her companions.

Frank Baum's literary Dorothy never speaks of rainbows, but color is a pervasive theme of this oft told tale. Color is one of the tools Baum uses to foreshadow Dorothy's transformation. The story is set in a gray Kansas farm. The prairie and plowed land are gray as far as the eye can see, as are Aunt Em's eyes and cheeks and Uncle Henry from his boots to his beard.

Their little one room farm house, once painted, has also faded to gray under the relentless onslaught of sun, wind and rain. The colorless farm inhabits a dualistic world of black or white in which feminine virtues are underappreciated and subservient to the masculine: mind reigns supreme over the body, head over heart, spirit over soul, "doing" over "being."

"When Aunt Em came there to live she was a pretty, young wife. The sun and wind had

changed her. They had taken the sparkle from her eyes and left them a sober gray; they had taken the red from her cheeks and lips, and they were gray also. She was thin and gaunt, and never smiled, now. When Dorothy, who was an orphan, first came to her, Aunt Em had been so startled by the child's laughter that she would scream and press her hand upon her heart whenever Dorothy's merry voice reached her ears; and she still looked at the little girl with wonder that she could find anything to laugh at." (Baum, p.2)

Without the feminine virtues of receptivity and joy in companionship, this masculine world of duty and hard work appears dull and lifeless. Dorothy's laughter, when playing with her little black dog, Toto, stands out in sharp contrast to her grim surroundings.

Having run to rescue Toto when the cyclone hit, Dorothy is unable to join her aunt and uncle in the safety of their underground shelter. She is, instead, transported on a whirlwind induced journey to Oz.

Emerging from the farmhouse after a rather gentle crash-landing, Dorothy beholds a lush landscape. She is met by the strange sight of three Munchkin men dressed in blue with bells on their hats and the Good Witch of the North, an old woman clad in a white dress decorated with stars. (Director victor Fleming took the liberty of merging her with Glinda, the young and beautiful Good Witch of the South in the 1939 MGM movie musical.) The bells are a call to pay attention, to wake up. The stars, perhaps, indicate that Dorothy's wish will come true, and her aged appearance might suggest that wisdom awaits Dorothy at the end of her journey since all the witches represent some aspect of Dorothy.

The fact that there are four witches, two good and two evil, is symbolically important as each represents a part of a whole, integrated self. Dorothy begins her journey when her house (a dream representation of self and feminine consciousness) lands on and kills the Witch of the East, representing ignorance and unconsciousness.

Dorothy is welcomed by the Good Witch of the North, an old woman robed in white and silver. This is the crone, the archetypal wise woman, a loving, all-knowing grandma. It is she who initiates Dorothy on the journey by handing her the witch's silver shoes (MGM turned them ruby red to contrast with the yellow brick road, thus losing some of their powerful symbolism).

The Good Witch offers her protection with a kiss, which leaves a mark on Dorothy's forehead. This precious gift is the breath of life, the imprint of spirit which will help ward off attacks from the Wicked Witch of the West. The wicked witches signify that which must die to allow for new growth. The Good Witch of the South is the young, beautiful counterpart to her sister of the North; together they represent what is good, true and beautiful in Dorothy.

To her amazement, Dorothy is greeted with joy and celebration for having slain the Wicked Witch of the East. She protests innocence until confronted with the legs and feet of the witch, sticking out from beneath her house, still clad in their silver shoes.

The Munchkins welcome her warmly, but Dorothy makes known her wish to return to Kansas. The Good Witch hands her the charmed silver shoes and tells her to follow the yellow brick road to the Emerald City where the great Wizard of Oz "may help you." She warns Dorothy that she must walk through a country "sometimes pleasant, sometimes dark and terrible." (Baum, p. 20) Nevertheless,, the Good Witch promises to protect Dorothy and kisses her gently on the forehead. Love will protect Dorothy from fear. This is something every truly conscious person knows. "Love casts our fear," St. Paul told the Corinthians.

To prepare for her journey, Dorothy first changes from her drab farm dress into her

14

Sunday best, a pretty blue and white checked frock. In dream interpretation, blue symbolizes communication and white, divine will, indicating Dorothy's willingness to follow her spiritual destiny, also known as The Way or Tao.* Next she adds her pink bonnet, symbol of the all protective mother's love.

Finally, Dorothy notices how badly worn are her black shoes. The worn shoes signify her current situation, and the fact that they are black indicates a lack of awareness. In order to move in a new direction she must shed this unconsciousness, these worn out shoes; she slips on the silver slippers which fit as though they are made for her.

With Toto at her side she takes her first step onto the yellow brick road. This little black dog, who symbolizes her inner yearning and instinct toward wholeness ("in toto"), will be the constant companion who keeps her from straying too far off course. According to the Tao, *"A journey of a thousand miles begins with a single step."*

---

* In Confucianism, Tao is the right manner of human activity and virtuous conduct seen as stemming from universal criteria governing right and wrong; a philosophy based on the teachings of Lao-tzu, 6th C., B.C.

Reflections - Chapter 1

1. Was there a time when your world appeared gray and colorless? Can you remember what it was like to live in a world where things appeared to be black or white? Has this changed? If so, how?

2. Do your "black shoes" pinch? What thoughts/concepts/perceptions or ways of being have you outgrown that need to be released so that you might exchange your worn-out shoes for shiny new ones?

3. The four witches represent parts of Dorothy; two must die that two might thrive. What in you must die? What is calling out to be nurtured?

4. Have you ever had a dream of dying/loss of something or someone? How did you feel about it? If you interpret it to mean some part of yourself is dying, what might that mean? Do these dreams inform us about our present fears?

5. What must die in your family/community/world in order for it to evolve to a world that celebrates goodness, beauty and truth?

FOLLOW THE YELLOW BRICK ROAD

A magical transformation is underway when Dorothy first sets her silver shoe upon that yellow brick road. Silver initiates a transfer of energy (Dale, p. 356) and symbolizes the feminine energy of Diana, goddess of the moon and the hunt. The silver shoes are Dorothy's link to the power of her soul.

When these silver shoes come into contact with the yellow brick road, which denotes the golden, masculine, spirit-filled energy of Apollo, Greek god of the sun, we know we will be seeing fireworks. One of the tasks Dorothy will face on this journey is that of balancing the masculine and feminine energies within her self. (See Chapter VII)

As Dorothy walks along the yellow brick road she comments to Toto on the unusual beauty of the green (symbolizing healing) fields and the blue (communication) homes of the Munchkins, who occasionally emerge to bow and smile at her. The bells on the Munchkins' caps jingle a call for her to continue to pay attention.

At one point she is invited to join a party with feasting, music and dance. Dorothy accepts the invitation. Sometimes when life seems especially challenging it is essential to slow down and enjoy the moment. The Munchkin, Bog, comments on the magical power of her silver shoes and thanks her for choosing to wear a blue and white dress, blue being the favorite color of the Munchkins and white, that of the Good Witch.

Bog evidently recognizes that Dorothy has selected these colors intuitively and affirms her for choosing to follow the path of truth and goodness that they represent. After spending a peaceful night with the Munchkins, a refreshed Dorothy resumes her journey toward the Emerald City though the Good Witch tells her that *"...you must pass through rough and dangerous places before you reach the end of your journey."* (Baum, p 25)

Despite the warning, Dorothy and Toto

start off on the yellow brick road. Yellow, besides representing the masculine energy of the sun god, Apollo, also is the color of the mental layer of the auric field (energy colors that surround the human body), thereby representing the intellect. In many cultures it also represents cowardice. Thus the stage is set for the appearance of both the Scarecrow, who needs a brain, and the Lion, who seeks courage.

After several miles, Dorothy stops to rest on a fence bordering a cornfield where she spies a Scarecrow. To her surprise, the Scarecrow begins to speak. Dorothy frees him from his perch on a pole, and he decides to join her on the road to Oz in hope of gaining a brain. While resting during a picnic lunch, the two friends hear a deep groan. Upon investigating, they discover the rusty Tin Woodsman. Dorothy oils the Tin Man, who joins the trek to Oz in search of a heart.

At this point the movie adds a dramatic flourish not in the original story by having the Wicked Witch appear to cast a ball of fire at the Scarecrow, forcing him to face his deepest fear. Fortunately, the Tin Man who, despite his belief that he is heartless, has a very caring heart, smothers the flames with his tin hat, and the journey resumes. Facing fear is essential to the continuation of the heroic journey.

Dorothy and her new friends venture into the dark woods and are startled by a deep growl, whereupon a lion bounds into the road and sends the Scarecrow and the Tin Man sprawling. Toto barks, the Lion roars, and Dorothy defends her little dog, calling the Lion a coward for threatening those weaker than himself. The Lion agrees and joins the travelers in the hope that the Wizard will give him the gift of courage.

When the Lion joins the journey, the symbolism of numbers becomes another indicator of change. In the study of numerology, the number three has an emotive, dramatic flair. As the number of the Trinity, it represents the cycle of birth, life and death as well as maiden, mother and crone. Since, embedded in every cycle is the element of return, the number three is considered to be inherently unstable, always yearning for the return, completion and wholeness.

Three is the number of the yang energy that is unstable until it is balanced by the feminine yin represented by the number four. Three is predictive of change as well as the dynamic force of creation. The triangle is said to represent both danger and opportunity. The number four, on the other hand, equals stability, completion and wholeness as well as the hard work, planning and self-discipline necessary to achieve these goals.

Interestingly, the study of numerology also associates each number with a color. Yellow is the color of the number three which, besides being the color of the road to Oz, is also the color of the third chakra represented by the Scarecrow in his search for knowledge and self-esteem. Green, a color so prominent in Dorothy's story that the entire city of Oz is bathed in its glow, is the color of the number four as well as that of the heart chakra represented by the Tin Man.

Finally, light turquoise blue is the color of the number five. This is the creative, impulsive energy that drives us forward beyond the instability of the three and the balanced energy of the four. Five seeks freedom, has excellent powers of observation and is the voice for the voiceless. It is, therefore, the number of the throat chakra represented by the Lion who seeks his voice and the courage to roar.

The use of numbers is subtle, but pervasive throughout *The Wizard of Oz*. Upon landing in Oz, Dorothy is met by three Munchkins plus one good witch. She soon discovers that there were four witches. However, her humble house (symbolizing her own self) has killed the Wicked Witch of the

East, leaving three witches, an unstable situation which demands resolution.

Just as the Good Witch's strong feminine presence balances and stabilizes the masculine energy of the three Munchkins, so Dorothy's feminine consciousness will balance the masculine energy of her three male companions. Of course, Dorothy also has an always present fourth companion, so much a part of her that he risks being overlooked. Toto often represents the unstable third point in a triad that propels Dorothy forward on her journey.

He actually initiates her journey by running away from the farm house, causing Dorothy to be caught in the cyclone. He also barks at the Wicked Witch, reveals the Wizard as a humbug and jumps out of the balloon's basket, forcing Dorothy to use her own power to find her way home.

Although Frank Baum does not develop the symbolic theme of numbers, his early introduction of triads with the addition of a fourth element prepares the reader to expect great upheaval in Dorothy's life while also presaging a hopeful outcome of balance and integration. Such is the quest of Dorothy, her friends and each of us as we journey toward consciousness.

Eventually the friends are led by a green

glow in the sky to the Emerald City. Emerald green signifies both hope and healing and the promise of new birth. These are powerful forces that are driving Dorothy and her companions onward despite their fears. As they approach the city gate, a watchman warns them of the great and terrible Wizard of Oz. Dorothy and her friends are forced to wear green glasses, which are locked on with gold chains, before proceeding further.

A bell at the gate is another warning to pay attention, but it is hard to see clearly when one is wearing colored spectacles. The foursome are so dazzled by the brilliance of The Emerald City and so awestruck by the reputation of the Great Oz that they, indeed, are unable to see clearly. They fail to see through his intimidation and are unable to recognize how he is using them for his own selfish purpose. He promises to grant their wishes only if they return with proof that the Wicked Witch of the West is dead. They will need more than the pretense and illusion offered by the green glasses to accomplish this life threatening task.

Dorothy and friends are filled with fear and sadness but, impelled by their individual desires, they wander westward toward the land of the Winkies. The way is hilly, rocky and rough. Eventually Dorothy, Toto and the Lion fall into a poppy-induced sleep. Though deep rest, and sometimes temporary unconsciousness, is often required for healing, to stay unconscious is fatal.

The Wicked Witch sends her wolves and crows to attack the travelers, but the Scarecrow strangles the crows and the Tin Man beheads the forty wolves with his ax, indicating that they already possess the traits they seek. Dorothy and her friends resume their journey only to be attacked by a swarm of black bees. Dorothy grabs Toto and snuggles up to the Lion, who is covered by the Scarecrow's straw. The bees break their stingers against the Tin Man and subsequently die.

After re-stuffing the Scarecrow, the friends venture onward. The furious Witch decides to use her final charm, a golden cap by which she orders her winged monkeys to kill the interlopers. The monkeys obey by scattering the Scarecrow's straw and smashing the Tin Man on sharp rocks.

Monkeys, bees, crows and wolves can have positive symbolic connotations, often representing a clever, industrious or playful nature. However, under the control of the Wicked Witch of the West, they have become instruments of terror, fear and death. If Dorothy can free these creatures from the Witch's spell,

26

they will emerge from shadow to light and become assets on her journey.

The monkeys recognize the mark on Dorothy's forehead, a reminder of the Good Witch of the North's protective kiss. Unable to harm one who is surrounded by this powerful love, they return to the castle with her and Toto, as well as the Lion whom the Witch wants to enslave. The Witch intimidates Dorothy into becoming her servant and tries to starve the Lion into submission, but Dorothy foils her plan by smuggling food to her imprisoned friend.

The Witch attempts to get the silver shoes from Dorothy, who is unaware of their magical powers but, nevertheless, refuses to surrender them. She holds tight to her power. In defending herself and Toto, Dorothy picks up the scrub bucket and tosses water (power pertaining to emotions/the unconscious) onto the Witch, who melts into a puddle which Dorothy sweeps out the door.

Here we have another symbolic gesture practiced by many cultures: the Japanese sweep out the old year; Christians and Jews clean kitchens of stale foods in preparation for Easter and Passover. Spring cleaning makes room for a breath of fresh air throughout the world.

Dorothy frees the Lion; the two of them free the Winkies who, in gratitude, help reassemble the Scarecrow and repair the Tin Man. Gifts of gold, celebrating one's best aspects or accomplishments, are given to Dorothy and her friends. Dorothy dons the golden cap which the Witch had used to command the winged monkeys. Now at Dorothy's command, they carry the successful adventurers back to the gate of Oz. Having gained in confidence by defeating the Wicked Witch, Dorothy and her friends confront the Wizard and denounce him as "nothing but a humbug."

The wizard tells the friends that his balloon drifted from Omaha to Oz many years ago and shares the tricks he has used to make the Munchkins believe he is a great wizard. The disillusioned friends are about to give up hope that this charlatan will be able to grant their wishes but, with a little ingenuity, he helps Dorothy's companions claim the truth of the traits they've shown throughout their journey.

Dorothy misses her chance to return to Kansas in the wizard's balloon, so she and her friends embark upon another perilous journey to seek the assistance of Glinda, the Good Witch of the South. (Baum, p. 84) With assistance from the monkeys, each arrives safely at their destination and Dorothy exclaims to Aunt Em, *"I'm so glad to be at home again!"*

An amazing transformation occurs in Dorothy as she follows the yellow brick road with her alter egos: the Scarecrow, the Tin Man and the Lion. At the start of the story she leaves a gray and lifeless world. At journey's end, she returns to the same place which has now become a fertile farm where she is welcomed with love and joy and all the colors of the rainbow.

Reflections – Chapter 2

1. What might be considered your masculine traits? Your feminine traits?

2. How do they balance one another?

3. What companions do you have on your journey who have helped you over the "dark and terrible" places?

4. What traits in your companions do you most admire?

5. Do your companions value the same virtues (wisdom, courage, compassion) as Dorothy's?

6. Do your companions encourage you to develop your own virtues?

THE TRANSFORMATION OF DOROTHY:
A Heroine is Born

So what exactly does it mean when we speak of the transformation of the Heroine's Journey? Although both classical mythology, popular folk and fairy tales and modern literature comprise a wide range of stories in the heroic genre, there are universal criteria that must be met.

Our protagonist must leave home, go on an adventure in which she faces her fears and fights her dragons with the help of companions, and return home with a new consciousness of her gifts and power and a willingness to share with her community.

Each heroic journey includes stages (usually seven) of progressing awareness. We will follow Dorothy through the seven stages of consciousness (archetypes) as described by Carol S. Pearson in *The Hero Within*: Innocent, Orphan, Wanderer, Warrior, Martyr, Magician and the Return Home.

When we first meet Dorothy she is, of course, an Orphan, living with her Aunt Em and Uncle Henry. She still has some of the characteristics of the Innocent who yearns for the delight of the Garden of Eden where life is lush and green and one is surrounded by love and care. This is an appropriate state for a small child, but it doesn't go over well in the world of adults. Aunt Em is startled by Dorothy's carefree laughter and, indeed, wonders what she can find to laugh about. Dorothy must escape this gray, joyless world in order to breathe life into her soul. The cyclone is her call to consciousness.

As the cyclone carries her away from the only home she can remember, Dorothy is thrust feet first into the Orphan archetype. Since the Orphan has not been well nurtured, there is a certain innocence or naivete in her personality makeup. While initially charming (isn't she cute

34

in that little gingham dress and pink bonnet?), such naivete doesn't prepare one well for the long journey and challenges to be met along the way.

Feeling like the Orphan after the Fall from Eden is a difficult place to be. The world is seen as strange and dangerous and resources insufficient. The dominant emotion of this worldview is fear, and its basic motivation is survival. (Pearson, p.27) Our heroine must move through this phase and experience her fear of powerlessness and abandonment as she journeys toward consciousness.

Fortunately, the Good Witch of the North and the Munchkins show up to help her find the way home. She must learn to hope and trust again in order to achieve her wish of returning to Aunt Em.

Dorothy willingly sets off on the yellow brick road, despite some trepidation, accompanied only by her black dog, Toto, and, of course, the silver slippers. In dream analysis, dogs typically symbolize devotion and protection, but they can also represent one's unconscious urges and instincts.

Toto, like the many pets pioneer women adopted, both for protection and to stave off loneliness when neighbors were miles apart, does offer Dorothy both comfort and protection (he attacks the lion, the witch and the wizard). He also represents the healthy instincts for self preservation with which Dorothy will need to connect in order to save herself from the power of the Witch and find her way home.

It is his playfulness and mischief that get her caught up in the cyclone and also cause her to miss the balloon ride back to Kansas. Both "happy mistakes" are essential for the successful completion of the heroine's journey.

Initially, Dorothy wanders along the yellow brick road, uncertain which direction to go, when she approaches a fork in the road. The "fork in the road" metaphor indicates a life changing choice. It has been written about most notably by Dante in **The Inferno**:

> *Midway in our Life's Journey, I went astray from the straight road and woke to find myself alone in a dark wood. How shall I say what wood that was! I never saw so drear, so rank, so arduous a wilderness. Its very memory gives a shape to fear.*

Poet Robert Frost describes this dilemma in **The Road Not Taken**:

> *Two roads diverged in a yellow wood And sorry I could not travel both*

And be one traveler, long I stood
And looked down one as far as I could to
where it bent in the undergrowth;
Then took the other...
Two roads diverged in a wood, and I-
I took the one less traveled by,
And that has made all the difference.

It is at this fork in the road that Dorothy meets the first of her three companions, the Scarecrow, who tells her that either choice will lead her to her destiny.

Companions are essential on the Heroine's Journey. Not only do they offer comfort and support, but they also represent the developing characteristics of the Heroine. In order to successfully meet her challenges and reach her goal, Dorothy must learn to think clearly, love unconditionally and develop the indomitable courage that results from compassion, all qualities she will absorb from her beloved companions as she grows from one stage to the next on her journey.

She will, like all heroines, pass through the **Victim/Martyr** (Tin Man) stage several times and be rescued by her friends. She will even let herself be intimidated by the Great Oz the first time around. However, she will not be deterred from the role of the searching **Wanderer**

(Scarecrow) as she steadfastly pursues her goal, even in the face of great danger.

She becomes the **Warrior** (Lion) as she confronts the Wicked Witch of the West to save both herself and her friends. Moreover, she subdues her opponent (slays her dragon, in hero's terms) not with sword and violence, but with a splash of water which represents the unconscious, and thus the power to connect to the deep inner emotions of one's true self. Dorothy has become the good witch who works magic by connecting to her spiritual essence. We will continue to explore this progression through the stages of the Heroine's Journey in subsequent chapters.

Read as a fairytale, Dorothy becomes the good witch who defeats the Wicked Witch of the West with magic. Read as an allegory, Dorothy, by connecting to the spiritual essence of her true self, has the grace of the universe at her finger tips. It is this unconditional love of Spirit which washes away ego: the life-denying-induced fear as represented by the Wicked Witch.

Part of the magic in Baum's story is that it can be read and enjoyed on so many levels. It is first and foremost, an adventure story: a tale of a young girl's growth and survival against difficult odds which gives it a universal appeal. It is also fairy tale and allegory as well as an

38

archetypal adventure story that taps into our shared collective unconscious which knows that each of us must take this journey along the yellow brick road.

Dorothy's new-found sense of self allows her to save not only herself and her companions, who represent parts of her self, but she is also able to do all the creatures of Oz a great favor by freeing them from the Witch's abusive power and releasing them from fear. She allows the inhabitants of the Emerald City to become more conscious as they remove their tinted glasses and say goodbye to the Great Oz, who ruled through intimidation and deception.

Though praised as a heroine, Dorothy chooses to return to Kansas, where her newly discovered wisdom, courage and ability to love will turn the gray landscape into a rainbow of vibrant colors. Each of these virtues is represented by her companions on the journey, the alter egos who are Dorothy's internal masculine helpers. Dorothy's innate feminine strengths will blossom to the extent that she develops and nurtures the masculine side of her personality; we observe these two parts begin to complement one another as her story progresses.

Reflections-Chapter 3

1. What aspects of your life so far have prepared you for the current challenges you must face?

2. Can you think of any "Happy Mistakes" that have changed the course of your life and, while initially unsettling, turned out to be good for you?

3. Name a time when you felt powerless and a time when you felt strong or powerful.

4. What dragons have you fought? What strengths have you discovered in yourself through dealing with adversity?

5. Name a cyclone/tragedy/adversity in your life that pushed you to a new level of awareness or discovery, a new level of strength or understanding regarding this issue.

THE THREE COMPANIONS

 As mentioned in the last chapter, companions are essential to the successful completion of the Heroine's Journey, and Dorothy is lucky to be accompanied by three very special companions, besides her guardian, the little black dog, Toto. In a woman's dreams, a *"...helping man represents an unknown helping part of herself."* (Clift, p.157)

The Scarecrow, the Tin Man and the Lion symbolize the parts of herself that she will develop and strengthen, as she journeys along the yellow brick road, in preparation for confronting her own shadow and ego-induced fear in the form of the Wicked Witch of the West.

"If I only had a brain": The Scarecrow considers himself to be a brainless nincompoop. Nevertheless, by virtue of the fact that he has been immobilized on a pole his entire lifetime, however brief, he has had the opportunity to reflect on his strengths and weaknesses. He knows enough that, to pursue his search for wisdom and self-knowledge, he must do more than talk.

He must get down off his pole and walk the walk, experience and interact with the world around him. Learning can't happen in isolation, nor will it occur while the Scarecrow is paralyzed by his own insecurities and obsessing over his own deficits. It's only by letting go of this perceived sense of littleness and focusing on the welfare of his friends that he is able to connect to the loving intelligence of the universe.

Gradually, his innate intelligence surfaces. He asks Dorothy to free him from the pole and reassures her that, no matter which fork in the road she takes, it will be the right one. We all get home eventually. Gaining in confidence as he focuses his intention on the goal of receiving a brain, the Scarecrow becomes adept at problem solving.

It is he who suggests they use the Lion to leap the gap in the yellow brick road and then warns his friends of the dangers of the poppy fields. The movie version enhances this aspect of the Scarecrow's personality so that, when the Wizard eventually grants him a diploma, it is simply a symbol, a sign of his innate intelligence. **"You Gotta Have Heart":** Once Dorothy and the Scarecrow oil and liberate the Tin Man, who is under the influence of a spell, he expresses his desire for a heart. *"Once I had brains, and a heart also; so, having tried them both, I should much rather have a heart, for brains do not make one happy."*

In Frank Baum's book, the Tin Man demonstrates his ability, not only to love and care for his friends, but also his courage in using his ax to protect them from attack. The movie builds on this theme by making the Tin Man so sensitive that he frequently cries when overcome with emotion.

The movie suggests that the Tin Man runs the risk of rusting. In fact, tears are healing, a lesson Dorothy has yet to learn. Real love, while often accompanied by pleasurable feelings, is a deep-seated compassion that grows out of steadfast commitment to the well-being of self and others. During the journey down the yellow brick road the Tin Man's heart expands and his ability to love both himself and others grows so much that, by the time the friends must go their separate ways, he laments, *"Now I know I have a heart because it's breaking."* (1939 movie)

Courage: stout-hearted: The Lion believes he is lacking in courage and indeed, behaves in a cowardly fashion by bullying the weak. Facing their fear, Dorothy and Toto call his bluff. At this point he certainly could not be called a "king of the forest." He is, despite his physical strength, the weakest of his companions, out of touch with his true nature, lacking in confidence and self-control. Nevertheless, like the others, he will be transformed by their journey. Soon he will exhibit all those traits we associate with courage.

In fact, shortly after joining Dorothy, the Scarecrow and Tin Man, he exhibits a bold confidence when he transports his friends one at a time across a wide ravine. The next hazard to confront the adventurous foursome is a field of poppies. Aware of the danger, the Lion tries to race through it, but is eventually overcome. As the Lion intuits, the poppies do indeed pose a huge threat. They represent the opiates, imposters that masquerade as substances which enhance the senses but, in fact, dull them to the point of unconsciousness and even death.

Our friends risk having their entire journey aborted if they cannot escape this hazard. Fortunately, the Lion is rescued by friendly field mice who symbolize the minor irritations, small fears and worries which tend to

46

gnaw away at us and must be confronted and mastered if we are to grow in consciousness. Having practiced patience in the face of difficulties on the journey, the Lion is able to be resolute and brave in refusing to be cowed by the Wicked Witch, despite her attempt to starve and threaten him into submission.

On his return to Oz, he confronts the Wizard with a stout heart that has grown out of his compassion, not just for his own frightened self, but also for his friends and the other oppressed creatures he has met along the way.

The Lion is the first of Dorothy's three companions to show signs of integration. Early in the story his actions indicate that he does, in fact, have the courage he seeks as he helps Dorothy confront dangers along the way. His recognition of these dangers and the care with which he seeks to shepherd his friends through them reflect aspects of the heart and brains sought by the Tin Man and the Scarecrow. They, in turn, are beginning to exhibit more signs of courage. The head, the heart and the hands are learning to work together.

Dorothy and her friends began this adventure together agreeing to collaborate so that they each might achieve their individual goals. As the journey proceeds, their union evolves into one of mutual cooperation.

Collaboration is the work of the head and the ego. It is driven by what is the perceived good of the individual. Cooperation is the work of the heart. It is fueled by the perceived good of the community. In rising above individual vanity, it defeats the ego.

> *"In every cooperative labor shines the flame of love and sacrifice, solemnity and perseverance, endurance and balance. Great is the beauty of the spirit of cooperation...The vision, or the purpose, of the cooperating members will charge each one of them with its fire and magnetism and will make people understand each other, respect each other, and cooperate with each other."* (Saraydarian, p.274)

It is important to remember that cooperation is not the only work of the heart. Dorothy must work hard to earn her way home, but part of her task is to find balance between work and play. Without joy the journey is pointless. Dorothy does take time to enjoy the beauty of the land and find joy in the company of her friends. This ability to go with the flow and follow her heart will serve her well when she confronts the fearful loneliness and separation in the witch's world.

As the three companions join in a

48

cooperative effort to defeat the Wicked Witch of the West they become stronger. Their strength and their ability to confront the ego-induced fear, which is fed by a sense of separation, loneliness and powerlessness, increase as, together, they focus their energy on a common goal.

Courage is both the driving force and the result of the integration toward wholeness. The three, though remaining separate personalities, will become one as they unite in Dorothy. One way of understanding this concept is by looking at the development of the energy centers in Dorothy as represented by her companions.

Reflections – Chapter 4

1. The Scarecrow: Do you know someone you would describe as a seeker of wisdom? Who has encouraged you to seek wisdom? Does amassing knowledge make one wise? The Scarecrow wants a brain and becomes wise and confident. How?

2. The Tin Man: Have you been the recipient of unconditional love? What does that feel like? When have you been most able to love unconditionally?

3. The Lion: Give an example of a courageous act. Have you personally witnessed or been involved in either courageous or cowardly behavior? Describe.

4. Describe a time when you collaborated with others as well as a time you worked in cooperation. How did the two activities differ?

CHAKRAS AND ARCHETYPES-
OH MY, OH MY!

What is the energy that is evolving as Dorothy and her companions journey down the yellow brick road? The body, like all life, is pure energy molecules comprised of atoms made of neutrons, protons, electrons and infinitely smaller particles moving faster than the eye can see. This energy flows throughout the body at different speeds.

Eastern medicine has for centuries acknowledged the flow of energy through a network of meridians. Traditional Chinese doctors have been trained for over six thousand years to heal the body by balancing the flow of chi using acupuncture and acupressure to remove energy blocks.

This energy collects at seven major

centers along the spinal column called chakras (Sanskrit for spinning wheels of light). Each chakra governs specific physical, emotional and mental functions of the human body and serves as an entry way to the related layer of a person's aura, the energy field that surrounds the body.

The seven chakras from the base of the spine to the top of the head are: the root, sacral, solar plexus, heart, throat, brow and crown. Each governs specific organs and physical systems as well as related emotional and mental states.

The first or **Root Chakra** regulates our relationship to our tribe/culture/religion or extended family. Dorothy permanently alters the energy in this chakra when she leaves the familiar old gray Kansas homestead and sheds the archetype of the Innocent for that of the Orphan.

As an Orphan she has much to learn. She wakes up to a strange new world, a country sometimes "dark and terrible." She must digest all this new information and discover how to nurture, care for and protect herself. This is the work of the second or **Sacral Chakra**. It governs the lower digestive organs and the nurturing, creative aspects of self love.

The next three chakras are represented by

54

Dorothy's three companions. The Scarecrow's challenge is that of the **Solar Plexus Chakra**; the Tin Man's, the **Heart Chakra**, and the Lion's, the **Throat Chakra**.

<u>**The Solar Plexus Chakra**</u>: The Scarecrow's challenge is to develop this third chakra. The Solar Plexus Chakra overseas the major digestive organs: liver, pancreas, spleen and gallbladder. These organs govern our ability to protect ourselves by absorbing new ideas and expressing enthusiasm-the "gut" reaction to life.

It is this energy center which helps us deal with issues of power and esteem, struggles with authority, aggressive tendencies, rage, anger, depression and digestive complaints. Because this is the chakra governing will power, it is also the source of energy we can tap for dealing with confusion, worry, control issues and addiction.

The solar plexus serves as the gate or entry way to the third level of our energy field. This mental level, seen as a yellow band of light, represents the problem solving power of intelligence. The ability to think clearly is critical to our functioning in the world. This ability is what the Scarecrow is seeking and why he has to get off his pole and engage the world to find it.

Even though his unused muscles are

weak, his posture floppy and his first steps tentative, it is essential that he take that first step. Interesting that he chooses to take those first steps on a "yellow" brick road. He, like Dorothy, will have much to digest before they can "gut it out" as they face adversity. These tentative first steps will grow stronger until, arm in arm with the Tin Man and Lion, they will be singing as they dance down the yellow brick road (movie version). They will also learn that the intelligence of the brain must be tempered by the compassion of the heart to produce the wisdom we need to govern ourselves and others responsibly.

Before Dorothy can reach her goal she must, like the Scarecrow, rise above her immediate self-interest and see clearly, not just with her two physical eyes and the little gray cells of her brain, but from the center of her heart. With this larger perspective she will be able to see that what benefits one, benefits all.

The Heart Chakra: The Tin Man's challenge is to develop the Heart Chakra, which governs diseases of the heart and circulatory system as well as breathing and immune failure problems. This energy center helps us become "unstuck", just as the oilcan helped the Tin Man be able to move again.

The heart's task is to open wide, to reach beyond duality to harmony by balancing perceived opposites such as shadow and light, masculine and feminine, mind and body. This wide open heart feels compassion for self and others, relaxes into acceptance and finds contentment in connection to what is real and true.

The work of this fourth chakra is to rise above the dictates of the ego, which is so important to the developments of the lower chakras. The release of the ego, and its pervasive tendency to pass judgment, allows for the birth of compassion. Compassion is accompanied by the virtues of gratitude and forgiveness, which free the heart to move forward on the journey.

Having grown rusty while frozen by the witch's spell, the Tin Man is unable to express the gestures of giving and receiving love and affection. Until Dorothy oils him, he can't even cry. He is unbalanced, but eventually he will become more integrated. He and his friends will share their strengths as they move forward with a common purpose. They finally unite and speak with one voice during their second visit to the Wizard; their roar will shake the world.

The Throat Chakra: The Lion's task is to

develop courage, the virtue associated with the Throat Chakra. Courage is also a gift Dorothy must give herself for, without this virtue, she lacks the strength to connect to her true self, that divine power within that will allow her to return home. This is the power and the grace of the 5th chakra, the Throat Chakra.

It comprises the thyroid gland, which regulates our energy. It also includes the ears, a critical component in our ability to learn from and connect with others, to experience the beauty of the sounds of the earth, and to understand that we are not alone. Teeth, so important to digesting, nurturing, growth and health are governed by the 5th Chakra. Can't you just see the Cowardly Lion, his teeth chattering with fear?

Nevertheless, as the journey progresses we can imagine him doing less grinding and gritting as his courage grows and he girds for battle. He claims the audacity to stand up and speak out for what he holds dear. He will be rewarded by seeing fear melt away in the face of truth.

The Throat is the chakra of compassionate commitment and the courage that flows from it. It also holds the energy we use in judging and criticizing ourselves and others-the opposite of compassion. Judging causes stiff necks and sore throats and strained relationship. Compassion relieves these pressures.

Practicing compassion, as Dorothy and her friends learn, allows us to honor and share our feelings, to speak our truth tempered by loving kindness. This ability strengthens our connection to our true self, our divine nature. When we develop our 5th Chakra our true creativity emerges, and we are able to claim our title of co-creator with God. We are on the way to making our universe a more beautiful place. We are on our way to enlightenment. We are on our way home. Like Dorothy, we will return home and wonder why we ever felt the need to leave home in the first place.

Before Dorothy can complete the final stages of her journey, she must also open and strengthen the 6th and 7th chakras. The 6th Chakra, often called the 3rd Eye or Brow Chakra, connects us with our intuition and is supported by all the chakras below it along the spine. The ability to tap into the powerful feminine energy of the 6th Chakra is critical to Dorothy's success in defeating the Wicked Witch of the West.

Only after she has strengthened and opened Chakras 1-6 is she able to fully utilize the power of the 7th Chakra, the Crown Chakra, which is the connection to her Divine Self. Now she can return home, bearing her gift-a new understanding of the goodness, truth and beauty which comprise her True Self. Looking at herself and her world with new eyes will transform Dorothy's entire life.

Reflections – Chapter 5

1. The **Root Chakra** governs our relationship with extended family and the larger community. Have you ever felt the pain of being isolated from others? What have you found helpful in healing this pain? Are you able to stand your ground when challenged? Do you feel safe and secure, healthy and wealthy? Do you sometimes feel overwhelmed with fear and anxiety. Are you able to be still, present in the here and now?

2. The **Sacral Chakra** involves digesting new information, learning to nurture and love oneself and fostering creativity. What happens when you fail to nurture yourself? Do you set healthy boundaries? Can you say "No"? Do you make room for pleasure and excitement in your life? Can you express a wide range of emotions? What is it like to have a creative endeavor frustrated? Are you comfortable with change?

3. The Scarecrow represents the **Solar Plexus Chakra**. Have you ever made a decision based on insufficient knowledge? Does following your "gut instinct" usually work out well for you? Recall some of your best decisions. Did critical thinking influence your choice? Do you feel confident and energetic and have a positive sense of self? Would you describe yourself as spontaneous and playful?

4. The Tin Man represent the **Heart Chakra**. What helps the Heart Chakra become "unstuck" and free to love unconditionally? Has some person or event helped you become less critical/more compassionate? What role do gratitude and forgiveness play in that movement?

5. The Lion represents the **Throat Chakra**. Do you find it easy to speak your truth? Have you ever been criticized for doing so? Who supports you in roaring out against injustice? Are you courageous enough to follow your best interest regardless of what others might think?

6. Do you tend to have a typical response to adversity- perhaps anger or withdrawal? If so, can you utilize your **Brow Chakra (3rd eye)** to visualize another way of being-perhaps perseverance or humor? Are you able to focus on one task at a time as Dorothy learned to do? Have you found your own dreams or intuition helpful in problem solving?

7. Do you have an active **Crown Chakra?** that is open-minded and comfortable questioning traditional beliefs? Have you had an experience, similar to Dorothy's of "returning home" with a stronger spiritual connection or a new mastery or piece of wisdom you longed to share?

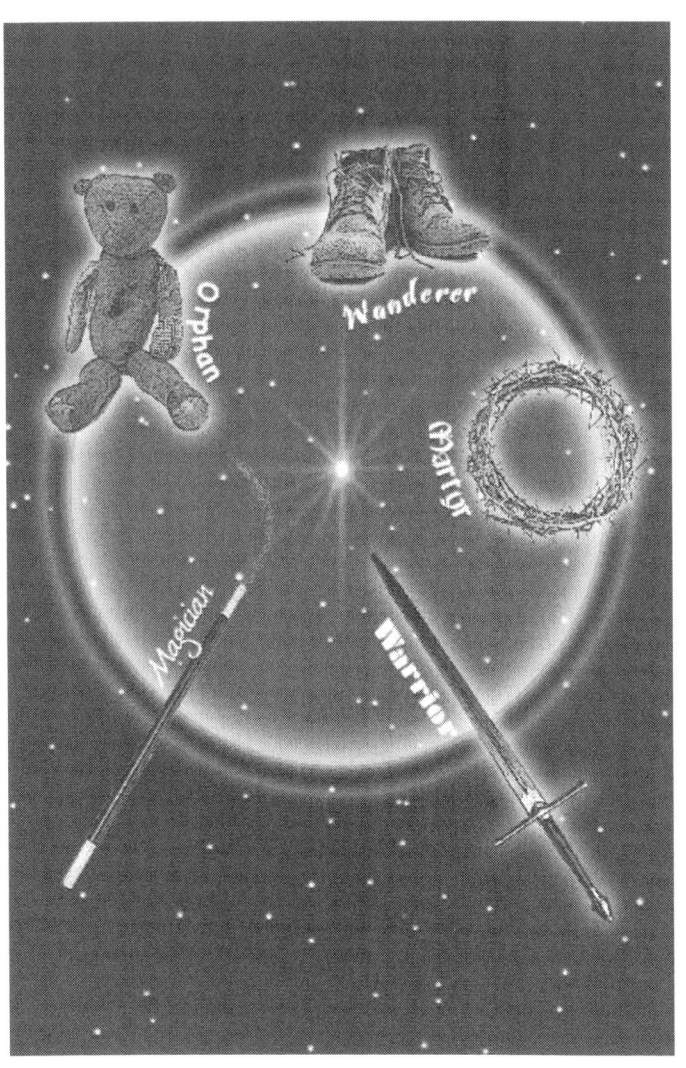

Orphan

Wanderer

Martyr

Magician

Warrior

ARCHETYPES OF THE HEROINE'S JOURNEY

Being forced to leave home and go on a long journey with the goal of returning home again, has immersed Dorothy in the feminine version of the heroic journey. The heroic journey is a progression through various archetypal personalities and related challenges.

Dorothy's story is especially powerful and universally symbolic because each chakra corresponds to one of the archetypal patterns that she manifests on her journey. Archetypes are amalgams of characteristics that define different phases of psychological growth; they are full of power and energy, encompassing both creative and destructive potential. As mentioned in the prologue **Dorothy and Friends**, the stages of the heroic journey vary from myth to myth and author to author.

Psychologist Robert Johnson, authors Joseph Campbell and C.S. Lewis and intuitive healer Caroline Myss have written scholarly works on the subject from diverse perspectives. In my previous book, *A Story of Grace*, I defined my heroic journey through cancer, using alternative medicine, in terms of Harry Potter's struggle to claim his inherent power in a Muggle world of unbelievers.

For this book, I have chosen to defer to Carol Pearson (*The Hero Within*) by describing Dorothy's progress from the stage of the **Innocent,** through the archetypes of the **Orphan, Wanderer, Martyr, Warrior** and finally, the **Magician**, before she returns home with treasure in hand.

The Innocent/Orphan

Dorothy begins with the task of the **Innocent**: the fall from paradise. Ironically, of course, Dorothy does fall, both literally and figuratively, as the cyclone releases her house onto the Wicked Witch of the East in the Land of the Munchkins. As the **Orphan** she must come to terms with a sense of powerlessness and strive to develop independence and survival skills. First and foremost she must learn to trust her own instincts; this is critical for discernment in learning to trust others, which is necessary to survive and thrive.

Many of our popular myths and fairy tales and even religious stories include the Orphan theme. In most cases this child is rescued by an animal (a wolf in Romulus and Remus), pharaoh's daughter (Moses) or a charming prince. Eventually Dorothy will find her rescuer within.

In the meantime, she is fortunate to make the acquaintance of the Good Witch of the North, who offers safety and support by handing her the charmed shoes and kissing her forehead, thereby leaving the protective mark of love. With this growing ability to trust in her own strength and the good will of others to meet her needs, Dorothy is able to feel the pain of her loss of home and family. As she releases this pent up emotion, energy is freed for her to continue on the journey that will bring her home.

The Wanderer

The next stage of our heroine's journey is as the **Wanderer**. Dorothy has Toto to help her cope with the loneliness of her separation from home. She also befriends various aspects of the masculine psyche, which Carl Jung, the Swiss psychoanalyst, terms the animus. Animus and anima (the feminine counterpart of a man's soul) have both positive and negative connotations. Dorothy must develop the positive traits of her animus in order to successfully confront the Wicked Witch of the West, who represents the negative ego-the life-denying part of herself.

The Scarecrow represents Dorothy's passage through the archetype of the **Wanderer**, the developments of her Third Chakra (power, will, self-esteem and entry to the mental level of the auric field). He also embodies the positive aspect of animus that includes discrimination, clear thinking, logic and analytical capabilities, mentoring and tutoring.

The Scarecrow's quest for a brain parallels Dorothy's need to develop her powers of discrimination so that she can discern which fork in the road to take, which battles to pick, the truth behind the lies and how to outwit her foes with skill over force.

Those familiar with the ancient Greek myth of Eros and Psyche, first recorded in classical Greek literature, might remember that discrimination was the virtue Psyche needed to successfully accomplish the first of the four tasks assigned her by jealous Aphrodite in order to regain paradise and return to Cupid. Dorothy's journey parallels the trials and tribulations of Psyche as she faces the challenges presented to her. Since this myth is referenced frequently, a synopsis follows:

Once there was a kingdom wherein lived a king, a queen and their three daughters. The youngest, Psyche, was so beautiful as to rival Aphrodite. The jealous goddess sent her son, Cupid, to dispose of Psyche, but he fell in love with her instead. Tempted by her sisters (those unloved parts of self we call Shadow), Psyche betrayed her love and was forced by Aphrodite to attempt four impossible, life-threatening tasks to win him back. Nature and the gods intervened to help Psyche and Cupid reunite.

Psyche's sisters represent the disowned parts of self which comprise our Shadow. When we engage the Shadow, we accept the call to consciousness. Psyche's path to awareness begins with the seemingly impossible task of sorting a huge pile of seeds by nightfall. Nature, in the form of an army of ants, comes to her aid. Nature, in the form of a man made from straw, will assist Dorothy in this Third Chakra task to claim the prize of the **Wanderer**, which is to take action, to initiate the journey toward a clearly seen goal.

We recall that Dorothy is a bit indecisive

upon meeting the Scarecrow. She sits down to ponder which way to go at a fork in the road. Her indecision might be the result of confusion, lack of energy, a lack of confidence, a tendency to blame her situation on others or any number of factors.

At this point she could refuse to continue her journey. She could stay stuck in the role of Orphan, return to the Munchkins and demand that they rescue and care for her. Instead she joins with the Scarecrow in his search for a brain. She elects to develop the balanced characteristics of the 3rd Chakra: responsibility for her own thoughts, feelings and actions, reliability, self-discipline and the will to succeed. These traits allow her to take the risks associated with the archetype of the **Wanderer**.

This phase of Dorothy's evolving consciousness will include an outward journey in which new friends are made, dangers met and mastered and foes overcome. It will also encompass inward growth as Dorothy develops and learns to recognize the positive side of her animus. Dorothy has emerged from the captivity of her little gray farmhouse to a bright and colorful new world.

The first job of the **Wanderer** is to see truly so she can think clearly. She must see the reality beyond the illusion in her search for truth

70

and also resist being deterred by real or imagined threats or those that think this journey toward self-discovery is pointless or selfish-especially for a girl! Women too often forego their journeys because their role has been defined as one of duty and nurturing others. Fearing the stress on their families, they opt out and thereby often cause greater harm with anger and resentment, the toxic blooms of their "sacrifice." Instead of becoming successful **wanderers**, they become trapped like **martyrs** in a Roman coliseum, eaten, not by lions, but by their own envy, jealousy, rage or cancers.

Dorothy, however, avoids these traps. She overcomes her initial loneliness and isolation by inviting three new companions to join herself and Toto on the yellow brick road. With an expanding ability to think clearly, she focuses her eyes on the road ahead, increasingly ready and able to meet the trials and tribulations that will come her way. Dorothy has made a commitment to learn to know her self. The clarity she gains on this journey toward self will earn for her the gift of community and prepare her for the task of the **Martyr**: loving others.

The Martyr

The task of the **Martyr**, learning to love and sacrifice for others, is also the work of the

4th or Heart Chakra. It is the quest of the Tin Man. The Tin Man says that he chooses to ask for a heart over brains, because "brains don't equal happiness." True enough, but one does need a certain level of awareness to be able to love another and experience happiness.

The Heart Chakra mediates between the lower (1st, 2nd & 3rd) Chakras, which relate to the body and earth energy, and upper (the 5th, 6th & 7th) Chakras, which have to do with personal creativity, insight and intuition and our connection with the divine. This middle ground is the abode of the **Martyr**.

Many of us, especially women who have experienced a culture that tried to force us into and keep us trapped in this role, have a very negative view of the archetype of the **Martyr**. It is seen as a state of loneliness and isolation, of angry, resentful caregivers trapped in a role that prevents true intimacy. We are so repulsed by this view of vigilant victim, who works so hard to please both Spirit and man, that we are unable to see the transformation that occurs when the positive aspects of this archetype are developed.

Redeemed **Martyrs** give from full, not depleted, cups. Therefore, the loving sacrifice they offer is freely given as an expression of genuine love and care. For Christians, this is the Easter Story, the story of Jesus' death and resurrection. Jesus left His heavenly home to model a human life of love and forgiveness that His followers might also learn the way home.

The hero/heroine who is operating from the Heart Chakra, in search of a heart like the Tin Man, or pursuing the archetype of the **Martyr**, is able to endure a life of hardship, trial and tribulation while maintaining love of life and also the capacity to care for others.

Mature **Martyrs** do not pass on, foist off or blame their suffering on others. Former president Harry Truman had a plaque on his desk saying, "The Buck Stops Here." The mature **Martyr** lives by the motto, "The Suffering Stops Here." Having learned to love and care for themselves as Orphans, and take responsibility for their choices as Wanderers, mature **Martyrs** are able to connect with the true self by giving to the universe, and their gift is love.

The decision to care is a choice to foster life and defeat despair. Just as the archetype of the Wanderer encompasses elements of the key virtue of faith, the **Martyr** elicits hope. Early Christian history is replete with stories of those who were martyred for their faith by emperors and local rulers who felt threatened by this new way of thinking and living in community.

Modern history brings us stories of those who live lives dedicated to the virtues of truth and justice and caring for those marginalized by society. Mother Teresa, Ghandi, Martin Luther King, Archbishop Romeo, Dorothy Day, Desmond Tutu, Sr. Dorothy Stang and Nelson Mandela are a few who have devoted their lives to others in recent years.

Commitment is an essential ingredient on this phase of the journey: commitment to one's goal (gaining a heart), commitment to facing unknown risks , commitment to the care and welfare of others and commitment to a certain loss of ego, the dying-to-self and surrender that sacrifice entails.

The journey through every archetype has its sticking points. Every one of us tends to stay overlong, bemoaning our loss of paradise as the **Innocent** or wanting others to care for, protect and rescue us from the **Orphan**age, and wouldn't it be nice if they could hand us a winning lotto ticket as well!

Perhaps we resist the **Wanderer**'s search for independence and autonomy, unable to stick with a single job for more than a few months or, conversely, become so identified with our job that we become stuck in the isolation of workaholism. The **Martyr** runs the risk of burnout and the resulting lack of empathy,

74

tempted to give up or try to escape. The **Warrior** archetype, represented by the Lion, must strive for balance between strength and weakness and avoid the trap of trying to control others.

The Warrior

Let's take a look at Dorothy's growth toward consciousness as she works through the archetype of the **Warrior** signified by the Cowardly Lion. At this stage of her journey, Dorothy is beginning to develop the energies of the 5th or Throat Chakra.

This chakra is ruled by the element of sound. Imagine a string of energy running through your core, the chakras strung like beads along its length from the crown of your head to the tail of your spine. Life events act like a harpist's fingers, plucking that string, striking a chord, which then vibrates with our inner truth. Facing these events gives encourages us to speak our truth and live in harmony with our core self.

Although the movie version of *The Wizard of Oz* plays up the cowardice of the Lion and turns him into something of a pussy cat, in the original story his first act is one of strength and courage as he ferries his friends across a huge abyss. The problem is, he didn't think of it himself. It was the Scarecrow's idea.

What the Lion needs to develop is a

thoughtful consistency toward using his gifts. Grounded in the compassion of the heart chakra, this growing commitment to himself and others will blossom into the courage required to speak the truth. The Lion will become a skilled communicator, able to listen to his inner self and also heed the hopes and dreams of others. The Lion will once again roar as king of the jungle, not as a bully, but with the voice of authority that comes when one has tapped into the true source of one's innate creativity. Now one can truly make a heartfelt "joyful noise unto the Lord."

In Yoga, the lion's pose, in which one sits on the haunches and roars, is recommended to strengthen the throat and protect against inflammation and laryngitis. It also helps get the creative juices flowing and release writer's block. As the Lion puts on the mantle of the **Warrior,** he will practice acts of compassion and commitment, and protect his friends in small ways until he finally earns his badge of courage from the Wizard.

Deep in our hearts we, too, know that this fight is our fight. Each day we must muster our own reserves of Brains, Heart and Courage to fend off that sense of littleness, unworthiness and Fear that the Ego sends our way to make us believe that we are separate from Spirit and unable to connect with our true self.

Dorothy, with the help of her faithful companions, is well on the way to being able to successfully confront the negative ego in the form of the Wicked Witch of the West. She is developing initiative. This is the experiential piece that the Scarecrow needs to add to his brains to gain wisdom.

Upon combining this newfound Wisdom with the Compassion of the Tin Man's heart and the Lion's Courage, Dorothy becomes very creative in overcoming the hurdles along her way. However, she has a few more challenges to meet before she is able to test her strength against that of the witch and, in so doing, claim the mantle of the Magician.

The Magician

Dorothy experiences the archetype of the **Magician** as she grows in her ability to manifest her dream. This is the energy of the sixth or Brow Chakra, often called "the third eye." The pineal gland, located within the brain in the "cave of Brahma" is central to the work of the Sixth Chakra which is perceiving and commanding. A pattern must be perceived and held in the mind before it can be commanded to manifest.

The Sixth Chakra assists the **Magician** in producing results outside the ordinary rules of life. This is the energy and the archetype Dorothy utilizes in following her intuition and in visualizing her return home, which becomes the guiding vision for her journey. As the **Magician**, she will manifest that vision into reality. Until that happens, like the **Magician**, Dorothy's faith and trust make it possible for her to wait for clarity, even when bad things appear to be happening. The **Magician's** question always is, "What can I learn from this experience?"

Dorothy is learning much from her experiences thus far. As she passes through the archetypes of the Innocent and Orphan, she discovers that, though the world can appear very scary at times, she has many resources available to confront whatever challenges she faces. She has brains, insight, intelligence and the willingness to engage the world one step at a time like her friend the Scarecrow.

Engaging the world with her increasing Wisdom is the first step to opening her heart and developing the Compassion of the Tin Man and the Courage of the Lion. These three aspects of Dorothy's masculine energy are becoming so fused together that, at times, it's impossible to sort one from the other.

However, despite her increasing wisdom, courage and compassion, Dorothy has still more to learn before she can don the mantle of the **Magician** and manifest her dream. Like every true hero/heroine, Dorothy must integrate and balance her masculine and feminine energies. These energies are depicted by the Yin/Yang symbol which introduces the next chapter.

Reflections – Chapter 6

1. The **Orphan** finds it difficult to trust herself and others. Who has offered you the safety and support you needed to grow in trust? Who has been your good witch? Why is trust essential for a successful life journey?

2. The **Wanderer** has to learn to cope with the loneliness of separation from home. He must discriminate between choices. What have you learned, what choices have you made, what foes have you outwitted that have moved you forward on your journey?

3. The **Martyr's** task is learning to love and sacrifice for others. Have you ever overdone this role and fallen into the angry resentment of feeling unappreciated? How do you protect yourself from this type of burnout?

4. The **Warrior** speaks truth with both courage and compassion. When have you spoken out of anger? What were the results? Can you think of a time that you addressed an injustice from a place of compassion? What response did you receive? Compare the two scenarios.

5. The **Magician** uses her intuition to form a guiding vision to manifest a new reality. When have you experienced this type of "magic?"

YIN AND YANG

Dorothy has come so far on her quest, but she must still balance and integrate the masculine strengths represented by the Scarecrow, the Tin Man and the Lion. The Chinese Mandarin symbol for Yin and Yang represents this balanced and integrated energy. Yang stands for the active male cosmic principles of sun and light. Yin represents a more passive, receptive female energy. Encircled, the symbol represents the oneness of all. These are the energies Dorothy must balance in order to fulfill her destiny.

Dorothy is not the Sleeping Beauty or Snow White who is rescued from the witch's spell by a handsome prince. Quite the contrary! She is the woman who claims the prince's best traits for herself, develops and integrates them into her own personality.

Like Beauty, she tames the Beast by insisting upon good manners, sharing art, music and literature and acts of loving kindness until he becomes civilized enough that they can live in the same house/castle/self comfortably. She does not rob him of his strength. It becomes transformed. It becomes the strength of the gentle giant that can co-exist with, and not destroy, Beauty. Thus Dorothy supports the Scarecrow in his search for wisdom, the Tin Man as he learns to love and the Lion as he grows in fearlessness. In doing so, she, too, becomes wise, loving and courageous.

Integrating this masculine energy (yang) is also the second task given to Psyche by Aphrodite.

After Psyche astounds Aphrodite by sorting a roomful of seeds in one evening, she is given an even more difficult task. Aphrodite demands that Psyche gather the fleece from a flock of golden rams. To approach the aggressive power of these rams head on would mean certain death. Fortunately, Psyche's intuition, in the form of a water reed, guides her to approach the rams after the heat of the day is passed, while they are

84

resting in their pasture. Quietly, without disturbing their rest, she gathers a small handful of fleece snagged on briars and brambles.

Psyche is wise to integrate this masculine power with discrimination. Too much would overwhelm her feminine identity (yin), and she might be tempted to use it in an oppressive, dominating or destructive way. Too little would subject her to the victim archetype and allow Aphrodite to destroy her. Finding just the right balance (after the heat of the day has passed) saves her from the path of self-destruction and assists her on her way to union with the beloved.

Dorothy, too, is learning the tricky art of balancing energies. Along with her friend, the Scarecrow, she is working to combine knowledge and experience which will allow her to grow in wisdom. The Tin Man represents her expanding heart, which grows stronger as she stays faithful to her commitment to her goals and those of her friends. Out of this heart-felt commitment will develop the courage to roar like a lion.

When Dorothy arrives in the land of the Munchkins, she expresses her wish to return home and is told to seek help from the Wizard of Oz. So initially, the Emerald City is her goal. It is only upon her arrival there and being fooled by that old charlatan, that she and her companions rethink their plan. They unite and agree upon a single new goal: to get the broom from the Wicked Witch of the West so that the wizard will grant their wishes. This single-minded, one thing at a time, approach to life is similar to Psyche's third task.

Having successfully sorted the large pile of seeds and gathered wool from the golden rams, Psyche is assigned a third yet more difficult task. She is to capture one cupful of water from the raging waters of the river Styx, which flows from a high mountain, descends into the earth and returns to its source on a never-ending circular journey. Every approach is guarded by monsters. Only by the help of Zeus' eagle is the task accomplished. The eagle has panoramic vision but, to help Psyche, it must focus on one spot in the river and take only one goblet of water.

As Dorothy is learning, those who cannot focus tend to get overwhelmed and lose sight of the rewards in a given moment. This task speaks to the virtue of focused discrimination. The balance point between scattered hyperactivity and apathy is this ability to do one thing at a time and do it well.

When Dorothy meets the Wizard for the first time, she naively thinks she can have it all:

—

a brain, a heart and courage for her friends and passage home for herself. The Wizard's demand that she kill the Wicked Witch of the West, though cowardly, causes Dorothy to let go of trying to be all things to all people and focus her energy on this single task. Frank Baum writes that Dorothy and her companions "sadly resolved to begin their quest the very next morning." (Baum, p.52)

There is sadness and a sense of loss involved in letting go of the pursuit of many dreams in order to pursue just one with the single-mindedness necessary for a successful outcome. However, this decision is essential to progress on the heroic journey. All strengths must come into alignment to achieve the desired outcome. Scattered energy breeds chaos. Thus head, hands and heart join with courage as the glue that knits them together.

This turning point is reached barely halfway into the original story. Dorothy has now partnered brains and experience and shown initiative in her quest for wisdom. Through companionship with the Scarecrow, Tin Man and Lion she has developed heart-felt compassion and the commitment to one another that leads to true courage in the face of danger.

While staying true to the best of her feminine nature (yin-that receptive, inner life that keeps her connected to the earth and calls her home), Dorothy has also developed the best of her masculine traits (yang-the action-orientated part of her personality that engages in the outer world). One task remains before Dorothy is strong and conscious enough to take back her power from the Wicked Witch of the West. This was the final task of Psyche: the journey to the underworld where one confronts one's shadow.

Reflections – Chapter 7

1. How have you tried to tame the beast within you?

2. When have you wished for a white knight to come to your rescue? How did that work out?

3. Are you aware of a specific time when you had to focus all available energy to accomplish a goal?

4. What is it like for you to be forced to discontinue pursuit of one passion in favor of another?

5. Describe a time when you chose to reclaim lost power.

WHAT THE SHADOW KNOWS

A key aspect of the heroic journey in every culture is the hero/heroine's confrontation with the shadow comprising those unrecognized, un-integrated aspects of the complete self. Hansel and Gretel wandered in their fairy tale forest; King Arthur's knights searched for the Holy Grail; the Bible tells how Jonah, after refusing God's call, spent time in the belly of a whale as did Pinocchio and his wood-carver father, Geppetto, two centuries later. Jesus descended into hell for three days after the crucifixion; Luke Skywalker, hero of the Star Wars movies, sees his own face reflected in the slain Darth Vader and Harry Potter repeatedly battles Lord

Voldemort in the recent British bestseller series.

Since confrontation with, and assimilation of, the shadow figures so prominently in the heroic literature of all cultures, it is worth a brief digression from following our heroine to discuss what the shadow is and how it develops.

The shadow comprises the traits and qualities we possess that we have disowned or failed to develop as we mature. It begins to form in early childhood when we are told "good girls (or boys) don't..." So the noisy/joyful, messy/creative, outspoken/reflective, gentle yet strong parts of self that are deemed unacceptable by our family, church or teachers fail to flourish.

Every healthy infant is born with the potential to relate to its environment equally from a feeling-thinking or creative "doing" capacity, whatever is most appropriate in a given situation. However, we learn early on that some responses are less acceptable or productive than others. Some families discourage asking questions or expressing certain emotions. Others proscribe the messiness essential to creative development.

Dorothy, as an orphan in a poor family, must find the nurturing she needs to grow into a responsible adult. At times she has perhaps been needy, insecure and afraid. Fortunately, she is journeying with companions who share these traits. They look at themselves mirrored in one another and develop the compassion for themselves and each other that will strengthen their courage and commitment as they confront their shadowy opposite in the Wicked Witch.

Moreover, Dorothy has her little dog, Toto, whose very presence reminds her that "everything" she needs is always with her, or within her, and accessible if she just stays conscious and avoids those poppy fields.

To successfully complete her task Dorothy must stay in the present, grounded in her power represented by the silver shoes. She cannot risk the diminishment that comes with focusing on past failures or fears of an unknown future. Confronting the shadow is a here and now proposition. To avoid this encounter is to give power to ego over self.

The story of Psyche, first written down in the classical Greek age, is our oldest recorded version of the heroine's journey to meet her shadow.

Aphrodite, distressed beyond belief that Psyche has successfully completed her first three tasks (sorting seeds, gathering golden fleece and capturing one cup of water from the River Styx), determines that she will not survive her fourth and final task. She demands that Psyche venture down to Hades and secure from Persephone, goddess of the underworld, a cask of her beauty ointment to be returned to Aphrodite.

Psyche climbs a tower, intending to jump to her death rather than embark on this fearsome journey. However, the tower (her inner strength supported by a legacy of wise women ancestors) instructs her on how to protect herself on this dangerous mission. The strength and wisdom she acquires during her previous tasks help her survive the perils of the journey.

She is on her way back when, distracted by curiosity, she opens the cask and is overcome by sleep. The essence of feminine power, secret of inner beauty and healing, is too much for one woman to try to capture for her own use. Love, in the form of Cupid, rescues her. The happy couple returns to Cupid's heavenly home where, in due course, their marriage is celebrated by the gods, Psyche gives birth to a daughter named Pleasure and, we presume, all live happily ever after. Johnson, **She**, p. 72)

With her commitment to seek and kill the Wicked Witch of the West, Dorothy has set foot on this same journey. It, too, is fraught with peril and, like Psyche, Dorothy must go prepared. She will utilize all the skills of her

94

friends and the gifts of the Good Witch to survive the deadly onslaught of this witch's forces.

The Wicked Witch does everything she can to disempower Dorothy. Her minions scatter the Scarecrow, topple the Tin Man and cage the Lion. She forces Dorothy into servitude and demands the silver slippers in return for her freedom, but Dorothy refuses to surrender her power.

Instead, Dorothy turns inward. She has already integrated the best attributes of her companions and claimed them as her own. Their temporary absence does not deter her from her path. With this inner strength anchored firmly in place, Dorothy has the fortitude to examine the here-to-fore unconscious aspects of her personality and claim those resources for herself.

She can look at the fears and insecurities, times of loneliness and doubts she may have experienced as an orphan. She can see how those very traits help her connect to, understand and have compassion for her three friends and be grateful for the love and loyalty that they now share.

"The task of the hero journey requires one to learn and experience not only one's strengths and

abilities, but also to learn one's weaknesses. The journey often entails the turning of what at first seemed to be an obstacle into an aid. When confronted, what appeared to be a dangerous monster or dragon may become the steed that bears one swiftly forward on the journey. In Jungian terminology this might be referred to as confrontation with and assimilation of the shadow." (Clift, p.91)

The value of the companions' timely intervention in helping Dorothy confront and assimilate her shadow cannot be under-estimated. The longer this shadow is kept hidden, the harder the work of exploring it. This is scary, dangerous and even life-threatening work.

It is walking into an abandoned mine in search of a lost vein of gold or silver, knowing that the roof could fall in at any time. It's exploring the locked room in Bluebeard's castle. It's confronting the stepmother and sisters in Cinderella, the evil witch/stepmother of Snow White, the beast, the giant, the dragon, the wolf in Red Riding Hood. Scary, indeed, but essential for growth and transformation. It is coming face to face with the Wicked Witch of the West.

The shadow holds the opposite of how we see ourselves. If we see ourselves as light, bright, sunny and happy-go-lucky, our shadow will look apathetic, aimless, dark or depressed. If we project an image of selfless generosity or collegiality, we might have a shadow that shouts, "Me, me, me!" The courageous soldier, policewoman or fireman will also have a weak or fearful side.

These shadowy aspects of our selves cry out for love, acceptance and attention. As we own these hidden parts of self, we become able to have compassion for self and for others. We also develop an appreciation for the gifts hidden in the shadow: the need for self-care first seen as selfishness; the urge for self-preservation beneath the anger; the sense of community with other human beings as we let go of arrogance and acknowledge our own weakness and fear.

Any part of our personality that we don't embrace will become hostile to us. The Wicked Witch has disowned her feminine side and it will defeat her in the form of Dorothy, a little girl with a bucket of water. The witch, who presents herself as a powerful entity to be feared, is really beset by her own loneliness, fear and insecurity. And so it is that Dorothy faces her own shadow when she comes face to face with the Wicked Witch of the West.

Reflections – Chapter 8

1. Are you aware of any part of yourself which you hid away as a child because it was deemed unacceptable?

2. Can you remember a time you first became acquainted with that unrecognized part of yourself called shadow?

3. Were you eventually able to acknowledge, love and accept that part?

4. What traits comprise your shadow?

5. Have you found it helpful to explore these hidden aspects of your personality?

THE WICKED WITCH OF THE WEST

FEAR!!! The Wicked Witch of the West is the voice of the ego that says, "You are alone; you are separate; no one will help you; I can overpower and kill you; be afraid, be very afraid." When Dorothy first set her silver clad foot on the yellow brick road, she probably would have succumbed to this negative voice. No doubt she struggled with the same character deficiencies as her companions: a lack of confidence, passivity, loneliness and even a certain arrogance and braggadocio.

However, during the course of their journey Dorothy and her friends begin to display a more positive, balanced sense of self that is reliable, confident, energized, caring and compassionate, able to speak the truth with conviction and courageous enough to face danger in the face of fear.

Dorothy is no longer the Innocent Orphan. She has taken the initiative of the Wanderer and gained wisdom. She has developed the compassionate, loving heart of the Martyr and the courage of the Warrior, who is willing and able to face fear. She has balanced and integrated the best of her masculine traits while remaining true to her feminine nature.

Moreover, she has explored her unconscious shadow side to discover hidden gifts and strengths while, at the same time, connecting deeply to all aspects of herself and forging strong links with her friends and, by extension, the rest of humanity.

She will not be swayed by the witch's fearful threats. She will not, under any circumstances, hand over her silver shoes. She will not give away her power in exchange for false promises. She is committed to staying connected to her true self. She has become conscious of the divinity that undergirds her humanity and nothing the witch can do or say can destroy that new found consciousness.

Although the story of Dorothy and her hapless friends is delightful and the 1939 movie comprises memorable music and lyrics, it is the specific ways in which the characters are transformed that continues to capture our interest. Would we have been so captivated had this foursome been seeking peace, joy and patience? Probably not; because, as valuable as these virtues are, they are not as helpful as wisdom, love and courage in subduing the Wicked Witch of the West, who symbolizes the destructive ego, with its abuse of power and tendency to make us feel separate and alone and therefore, full of fear.

Each character is clearly transformed by their journey, and they are also transformed as a whole. The Scarecrow has requested brains, but they all need the ability to think clearly and see through the humbuggery of the Wizard and the lies and wickedness of the Witch to the cowardice beneath.

The Tin Man has requested a Heart, which is the foundation of Courage. The French word "coeur", meaning Heart, is the root of our word "Courage" or stout-hearted. All four friends must learn to love themselves and one another, or they will never have the strength to complete this arduous journey and make their dreams come true.

Through sharing bread and adventure, pain and pleasure, they evolve to think as one.

This evolution has taken them from being four separate Innocents, who want others to "fix" them, to a unified whole that is able to love, care and have compassion for each of its parts.

From this compassion has emerged true Courage that, though recognizing the risks, is willing to confront evil for the good of all. There is a modesty and generosity of spirit in this type of courageous commitment that is far more powerful than the greed for power of the Wicked Witch. It also stands in sharp contrast to the excesses of the Wizard's palace in Oz. The sham palace of the sham Wizard vanishes when confronted with Dorothy's real presence and commitment to truth.

It is this deep love and compassion that Dorothy and her friends have learned to practice toward themselves and one another, supported by clear thinking and the Courage to speak their truth, that melts away Fear and its partner in crime, a sense of unworthiness and isolation.

Deep in our hearts we, too, know that this fight is also our fight. Each day we must muster our own reserves of Brains, Heart and Courage to fend off that sense of littleness, unworthiness and Fear that the ego sends our way to make us believe that we are separate from Spirit and unable to connect with our true self, God's beloved child.

Possession of the silver shoes, gifts of the Good Witch, allows Dorothy to retain her power over the Wicked Witch of the West. Let's take a closer look at the source of this power and what it means for the woman on the way home. As mentioned in Chapter 1, silver is the feminine link to the power of the soul. It represents the receptive, yin energy of the Diana, goddess of the moon and the hunt. This is the yin energy which is able to receive, listen, give, be still and simply "be."

These are invaluable gifts which, when combined with the best of her masculine personality, make Dorothy a living example of the reconciliation of opposites, of wholeness and integrity. It is this balance, wholeness and integrity which is needed to confront the negative ego in the form of the Witch which produces Fear by promulgating the false belief that we are not whole-that we are, in fact, separated, alone, lonely and on our own.

The Wicked Witch stands for power that is used in an oppressive, egotistical and destructive way. Her world, that of the negative ego, is impersonal and competitive rather than mutually affirming, nurturing and communal. The Wicked Witch is out of balance. She has too much fire energy. Having failed to develop her feminine side she has lost touch with her emotions (water) and is no longer grounded in reality (earth). Thus it is no surprise that, what leads to her demise, is a splash of water from a little girl standing firm in her silver shoes, sent her way by a tornado (air) and protected by the loving kiss (breath of life) of the Good Witch.

If we understand water as representing the unconscious (a typical interpretation in dream analysis), the fire and water analogy is filled with symbolism. Dorothy may be young in years, but her experiences with her companions have caused her to become more aware. This growing consciousness makes it possible for her to handle *"a bucketful of water"* (Baum, p 61) with ease.

The Witch, on the other hand, is out of balance, burning up with anger and rage-oppressive masculine energy unmitigated by any feminine counterpart. Hence, a bucketful of water is enough to totally extinguish her. She is completely overwhelmed by the emotions and feminine power which Dorothy wields so effectively. Dorothy becomes aware that the Witch and the Fear she projects are all an illusion and, with the awareness, the illusion goes out the door.

Up until the point where Dorothy actually throws water on the Wicked Witch it is touch and go as to who will win this battle.

Confronting the powerful negative ego with its deadly messages of guilt, separation and powerlessness is often a life and death challenge.

In the book, the Witch trips Dorothy and captures one of the silver shoes so, to an outsider, it appears as though the odds are even. However, for Dorothy, this is the straw that breaks the camel's back. This final insult releases all the pent up anger over the mistreatment of her friends and her own imprisonment. This anger at injustice gives Dorothy the energy to right a great wrong.

The Witch, of course, helped seal her own fate. Like each of us from time to time, she has failed to integrate her thoughts, feelings and life experiences as she journeyed on life's path. This huge weight of separated self drags us down like a ball and chain until it threatens to sink us. This weight made it difficult for the Witch to move out of the way of the water.

Dorothy, unaware of her latent capacity to save herself and make her dreams come true, had hoped for a savior or hero outside herself. Now she realizes it's "do or die!" Her anger allows her to harness the strength within and become her own rescuer. When Dorothy claims her own power her true self emerges, and she is assured victory over the witchy, life-denying, false self.

A powerful creativity erupts when our best masculine traits unite with the heart-centered feminine wisdom. This creative force inspires Dorothy to fight fire with water, the one element that can melt away the Wicked Witch. Evil is impotent in the face of this strong spiritual connection to the true self which knows that nothing can harm God's child and, therefore, Fear is always an illusion.

Noticing what a mess the melted Witch has made, *"Dorothy drew another bucket of water and threw it over the mess...swept it all out the door, and ran to tell the Lion that the Wicked Witch of the West was dead!"* (Baum, p. 61). The power of light defeats the darkness and love washes away fear. If hell can be defined as living in fear then, in destroying the Witch, Dorothy has, like Psyche, descended into Hades and returned with a deeper understanding of her power.

Reflections – Chapter 9

1. What is the biggest fear you have had to face?

2. What support did you have in confronting this fear?

3. Was this decision primarily driven by wisdom, compassion or courage?

4. How were you changed by this encounter?

5. As you fought this battle, did you feel more connected to others or more isolated.

THE RETURN OF DOROTHY

Dorothy's heroic journey is approaching completion. She left home to discover, develop and balance the best aspects of her masculine and feminine self. She confronted her shadow and successfully journeyed to the underworld where she slew her dragon. In the process, she learned that the very thing we most fear can prove to be that which pushes us forward on our spiritual journey home.

Now she must complete the third and final phase of the heroic journey: the return home with gift in hand. Despite her magnificent feats, there is still a part of Dorothy that yearns to be rescued, so back they head to Oz to hold the Wizard to his promise. When the Wizard acknowledges *"I am just a common man,"* the Scarecrow replies, *"You're a humbug."*

As the companions hear the Wizard's story, they grow disappointed and angry. *"I think you are a very bad man,"* says Dorothy. *"Oh, no, my dear, I'm really a very good man; but I'm a very bad Wizard, I must admit,"* replies the Wizard. (Baum, p. 75)

Nevertheless, though not a skilled magician, the Wizard is a kind and clever man, and so he gives the Scarecrow, the Tin Man and the Lion gifts that affirm their innate capacities for wisdom, love and courage. As for Dorothy, the Wizard plans to return her to Kansas through the air since *"We each came to this country by air."* (Baum, p. 81)

The Wizard and Dorothy spend the next three days making a balloon from three different colors of silk. Here come those unstable threes again. He cuts and she stitches. Dorothy is still designing her life from someone else's pattern. Green, as mentioned earlier, is the color of the Heart Chakra. It also symbolizes new growth, awakening, healing from the heart and integration. Unfortunately, this balloon will be filled with 'hot air', so it can't be Dorothy's vehicle for the journey home.

Once the balloon is inflated, the Wizard invites Dorothy on board. Although he is an unlikely hero, Dorothy still hopes the Wizard will be her "knight-in-shining-armor." However, her subconscious instinct, in the guise of Toto, jumps from the balloon, forcing Dorothy out, away from all that hot air. Dorothy's instincts (Toto) tell her that she must look inward to find her way home.

She will succeed on this last leg of her venture by reconnecting with her true self symbolized by Glinda. So off she goes to confront a new set of dangers on her way to the castle of the Good Witch of the South. This time her three companions, assisted by the winged monkeys, skillfully guide Dorothy through a dangerous forest filled with wild beasts and over rocky hills inhabited by unfriendly creatures.

It is at this point that the movie version differs most dramatically from Baum's story. Dorothy has another whole series of adventures awaiting her after she follows Toto out of that balloon. Having been blessed by the Good Witch of the North and having subdued the Wicked Witches of East and West, she must bring events to completion by visiting the South.

This is necessary for balance. Like any good shaman (Magician), Dorothy knows the importance of honoring the animal and spirit guides of all four directions on the medicine wheel (an artistic creation used by Native

American Indians to honor Mother Earth).

Surviving many more horrible hazards, the faithful friends finally meet the beautiful Good Witch of the South. Glinda congratulates Dorothy's three companions on their successes and commends their decisions to return as leaders: the Scarecrow to the Emerald City, the Tin Man to the land of the Winkies; the Lion to the grand old forest where the animals have asked him to be their king.

Glinda tells Dorothy *"Your silver shoes will carry you over the desert. If you had known their power, you could have gone back to your Aunt Em the very first day you came to this country."*

"But then I shouldn't have had my brains!" cried the Scarecrow.

"And I shouldn't have had my lovely heart," said the Tin Woodman.

"And I should have lived a coward forever," declared the Lion. (Baum, p. 95)

The heroic journey culminates in a gift for the heroine as well as her community.

Dorothy hugs and kisses her friends goodbye and thanks Glinda for all her kindness. Taking Toto in her arms she claps the heels of her silver slippers together three times. (It has to be three!) "Take me home to Aunt Em!" she exclaims.

Em is the universal consonant for the

word Mother. As such, Aunt Em represents the archetype of the Divine Mother. By returning home to Aunt Em, Dorothy is able to connect the two major aspects of her feminine self: Heroine (protective self) and Divine Mother (nurturing self). Incorporating these parts of self into her own soul allows her to form a healing energy so powerful that it transforms her entire world.

Suddenly, Dorothy is back on the farm in Kansas, but it is not the drab, gray place she left. There is a brand new farmhouse Uncle Henry built to replace the one removed by the cyclone. Uncle Henry is milking the cows and Dorothy sees Aunt Em running toward her. *My darling child!* cries Aunt Em folding Dorothy in her arms and covering her face with kisses. Dorothy joyfully allows herself and Toto to be embraced by Aunt Em, exclaiming, *"Oh, Aunt Em! I'm so glad to be at home again!"* (Baum, p. 96)

Dorothy is no longer the abandoned orphan, fearful and alone, needing someone to care for her. She has taken the "road less traveled" and journeyed inward to unite with her true self. Along the way she built a community that encouraged, nurtured and supported her as she met challenges, developed her gifts and fought her dragon. Now she returns home with a new appreciation of her own gifts and strengths and a deeper understanding of the joy and blessings of the community she left so precipitously.

Because Dorothy has been transformed, her old gray, barren world is also transformed. She sees with new eyes and what she sees is health, prosperity and love. Even the farmhouse, symbol of self, is brand new.

With this new vision comes the gift of leadership. However, unlike her three male companions, Dorothy will not rule over an outward kingdom. Hers is an interior reign. In this transformed kingdom she experiences a peaceful relationship of community with herself, others and the world at large.

This ability to unify her inner and outer worlds gives Dorothy a sense of autonomy and authenticity which allows her to bring light to the darkness both within and without. As such she can both give and receive the nurturing that will assist her ongoing growth.

Such vulnerability prevents arrogance and fosters a sense of humility and human connectedness that allows the hero to lead by virtue of example rather than force, ordination or election. Our heroine's joy and enthusiasm for life will serve as a beacon, a light in the darkness, which others will choose to emulate.

Of course, Dorothy, despite her incredible journey and amazing feats, is still a young girl with a lifetime left to live. She will at some point fail to stay connected to her true self. Once again she will have to embark on the heroic journey and face Fear. Over and over the Wicked Witch of the West will attempt to intimidate her into handing over her power, but Dorothy will never surrender to Fear.

She has become the Magical child with the redeemed qualities of the Innocent as described in **Sacred Contracts**. (Myss, p. 373) The Magical Child is both enchanted and enchanting to others. She sees the potential for beauty in all and also embodies qualities of wisdom and courage. She no longer needs to wear the silver shoes-they have become a part of her self.

She has built the Rainbow Bridge that connects the physical aspects of her personality to her Divine nature. Having walked this path home, she will never forget the way, no matter how distracted she may become at times. Deep inside, she knows the truth. She knows that the truth will set her free. She knows that love casts out Fear. She has moved from Fear to Faith and claimed her identity as God's Beloved, the Divine Child. This is the goal of the journey. She is already home!

Reflections – Chapter 10

1. Has there been a time when your nurturing self (Divine Mother) joined with your protective self (Heroine) to help you see your world through new eyes?

2. How does your view of the world change when you look through the eyes of the heart?

3. Have you personally had an experience of love conquering fear?

4. If fear is an illusion, why do you think so many people are driven by it?

5. What gifts do you have to offer the world as a result of your own heroic journey.

EPILOGUE

There was a time when relatively few men and even fewer women chose to embark on the heroic journey. However, the modern woman is better educated, has more freedom and is able to tap into a growing consciousness and support system that will give her permission to make this choice.

As I mention in the Introduction, I do hope that more women will choose to embark on the Heroine's Journey, strengthen their energy systems and embrace the archetypal challenges that will lead them to a new awareness of their abilities and the unique gifts they have to offer to their families and communities.

Many more of us are called to do this difficult work, to develop our individual potential in order to alleviate suffering and save our endangered planet. We are called to transform our society by shedding light on our individual and collective shadow to bring light to the world.

The work of transformation is most helpful if undertaken by someone centered in her own wholeness. This wholeness is the result of integrating all our component parts, claiming the **Wisdom, Compassion** and **Courage** of our own Scarecrow, Tin Man and Lion.

We are a spiritual people leading an earthly existence. Because we are temporarily separated from Home, fear is at the very core of all we experience. However, if we follow Dorothy in developing **Wisdom, Compassion** and **Courage** we will grow stronger each time we face our fear which seems to keep manifesting in so many different ways simply to allow us to practice letting it go.

Fearlessness, along with perseverance and constancy, are the virtues needed to open and strengthen the chakra energy system. It is this system that supports our search for creativity and passion in life. (Saradarian, *Healing*, pp. 127-131)

As I look back over my own life, I am simply astounded at the many guises of fear, some more intense than others, but each with its own level of anxiety and trepidation. There were early childhood fears as my parents battled life threatening illnesses; the low level fears of being "different" in school; the unknown of beginning university in a distant city; the challenges of marriage and the fears of separation and danger when my husband was sent to Vietnam while I stayed home with our two little ones.

There were the adjustments with each of our thirteen household moves, financial and health challenges and fears for our children as they negotiated life's ups and downs.

There were also those fears that surfaced symbolically in dreams as I struggled with wild animals, snakes and forces of nature that represented parts of my self which were either dying, struggling to survive or needing to be released. Difficult as these incidents were, they each made me stronger and more resilient, more able to respond to myself and others with love, empathy and forgiveness.

In retrospect it seems to me that my life has been a preparation for receiving the diagnosis of breast cancer in 2006 with a conviction that I could heal using alternative therapies, and then being able to move through that year long journey of healing with a relative freedom from fear. I discovered that one can only become fearless after having first confronted fear.

"When one has grown strong and wise enough, the warring elements which cost so much suffering and anxiety, will become complementary elements and produce the great work of art which is your own life." (Johnson, *SHE*, p. 80)

I believe one reason that Dorothy's story continues to capture our hearts and imagination, most recently in the sell-out crowds viewing "Wicked" on stage, is that our culture is also undergoing a shift from operating out of the Third Chakra to the Fourth. Our country and, perhaps, the world at large is on its own version of the Heroic Journey.

We are beginning to see this shift in our country's leadership with its focus on diplomacy and cooperation. We see it, too, in an increasing effort to speak out on behalf of the voiceless: housing for the homeless, protection for abused women and children, laws to protect animals from inhumane treatment and stronger anti-pollution measures. We are getting better at loving ourselves, our land and the creatures with which we share it.

In searching the news with a discriminating eye, it is easy to find inspiring stories of those who choose to offer a portion of their lives to fostering hope, the gift of the Martyr archetype. I think of those "Doctors without Borders" or others in medical, teaching, engineering professions who dedicate several weeks or months, often confronting great danger, to help lift others from misery. I know personally of many who travel to foreign countries to build homes, distribute food or transport medical supplies.

A recent PBS special interviewed a local Colorado woman who began a project, "Beads of Hope," that has allowed a village of 600 homeless Ugandans to own their own brick homes, grow their own food and train in a variety of small businesses. They have built a sustainable economy where their children are educated in an atmosphere of love and safety.

Quite a contrast to the violence and despair that had dominated their lives before this American woman, wearing the mantle of the Martyr, arrived with a loving heart filled with seeds of hope. Though I have never met this woman, this angel of mercy, I did see the light in her eyes as she talked with the women who were so proud of their new homes and flourishing gardens. Such love and joy!

And that is what it is all about: love and joy! The hard work of transformation, the entire point of the Heroine's Journey, is lost if there is no joy. Just as we seek to balance the work of head, heart and hands and integrate Brains,

Love and Courage, so, too, must we balance work and play. Our souls cry out for us to celebrate life, to stop and smell the roses and find wonder in the surprises life brings us with each new day.

As we begin to operate from the Heart Chakra by demonstrating care and compassion for ourselves and others, this expanded energy of devotion will bring harmony to us as individuals and to our societies. Relationships in our families and communities will become more harmonious. As we cease polluting our environment with negativity such as anger, guilt and greed, and toxic chemicals, we will once again be able to breathe freely. With this new found freedom will come a decrease in asthma, allergies, cancers and other chronic disease.

When enough people begin to operate from the energy of the heart chakra, we will see a positive shift in societies throughout our world. Since green is the healing color of the heart chakra, we will truly become the "green" planet Mother Earth is meant to be. As I go to press, courage is breaking out all over the world: indigenous peoples are confronting corporations that pollute their land, air and water; courageous citizens are rebuilding after the devastation of floods, earthquakes and hurricanes, and the fearless young people of the mid-east are risking their lives to claim freedom after enduring decades of tyranny.

Our country, our world and our earth are crying out for healing and transformation. Those of us who choose to follow Dorothy on the Heroine's Journey are called to lead the way. Life is one long invitation to open our hearts, our minds and speak the truth with conviction as we continue to perfect our ability to love and forgive and embrace what comes our way with gratitude. In other words, life offers us a never ending invitation to FOLLOW DOROTHY on the Heroine's Journey.

The author would welcome comments to nancybattilega@hotmail.com.

NOTES OF APPRECIATION

I would not have written *Courage and Compassion: Following Dorothy* without the inspiration of my own Aunt Dorothy, who appeared to me in January of '08 and suggested the theme for this book. Dorothy Eachus was born into a family and raised in a culture that celebrated the intellect. Nevertheless, she chose to live from the heart, to live an unhurried life in which one is able to take time to smell the roses and wonder at a rainbow-colored world where others see only black and white.

I am very grateful for the thoughtful comments of all who read the draft of this book. My husband and daughter were the first to help me pull some loosely connected ideas into a more coherent work.

My greatest gratitude, admiration and respect go to renowned local storyteller and author, Cherie Karo Schwartz, who labored countless hours to help me turn a rough stone into a polished gem. She guided, perhaps prodded, me until the story I held in my heart emerged from a head filled with facts, allowing my hands to write a tale I hope all will enjoy.

Thanks also to published authors, Kathy Hendricks and Jean Dalby Clift, who both took time from their busy schedules to suggest corrections and additions and offer the professional advice so helpful in getting this work to press. Jean's psychological insights and Kathy's attention to detail have greatly enhanced the accuracy of this book.

Special appreciation goes to artist, Deborah Gotto, whose black and white illustrations set the tone for each chapter and help bring this story to life. Thanks also to Catherine Morgan, friend and fellow author, who introduced me to Deborah.

As every author knows, it takes a village to birth a book. Many thanks to all the friends in my book clubs, writer's group and Healing Touch community who shared their love and encouraged me to stay the course as I endeavored to write about how everything I know about life I learned from Dorothy in *The Wizard of Oz.*

The author would welcome comments to nancybattilega@hotmail.com.

BIBLIOGRAPHY

Baum, L. Frank. *The Wizard of Oz.* Illustrated by Charles Santore. (Jelly Bean Press, 1991).

Caprio, Betsy. *The Woman Sealed in the Tower: A Psychological Approach to Feminine Spirituality.* (Paulist Press, NY, 1982).

Clift, Jean Dalby and Wallace B. The *Hero Journey in Dreams.* (Crossroad, NY, 1988).

Crisp, Tony. *Dream* Dictionary. (Dell, 1990)

Dale, Cyndi. *Advanced Chakra Healing.* (The Crossing Press,2005).

Estes, Clarissa Pinkola. *Women Who Run with the Wolves.* (Ballantine Books, NY, 1992).

Green, Joey. *The Zen of Oz.* (Renaissance Books/St. Martins Press, NY, NY, 1998).

Heilbrun Carolyn G. *Writing a Woman's Life.* (Ballantine Books, NY, 1989).

Hover-Kramer, Dorothea, with Midge Murphy. *Creating Right Relationships: A Practical Guide to Ethics in Energy Therapies.* (2009).
Johnson, Robert. *He: Understanding Masculine Psychology.* (Harper & Row, NY, 1989).

_____. *She: Understanding Feminine Psychology*. Harper & Row, NY, 1989).

_____. *Owning Your Own Shadow: Understanding the Dark Side of the Psyche*. (HarperCollins, 1939).

Lagerquist, Key and Lisa Lenard. *The Complete Idiot's Guide to Numerology*. (Alpha/Penguin, 2002).

Lewis, C.S. *Till We Have Faces*. (Harcourt Brace, 1984).

Murdock, Maureen. *The Heroine's Journey*. (Shambala, 1990).

Myss, Caroline. *The Sacred Contract*. (Harmony Books, NY, 1981).

Nelson, Gertrud Mueller. *Here All Dwell Free*. (Fawcett Columbine, NY, 1981).

Pearson, Carol. *The Hero Within*. (Harper/Row, 1989).

Saradarian, Torkom. *Dynamics of the Soul*. (T.S.G. Publishing Foundation, Inc., Cave Creek, AZ, 2001).

Zweig, Connie and Jeremiah Abrams, ed. *Meeting the Shadow for the First Time*. (Tarcher Putnam, NY, 1991).

16829846R00073